Emotional Abuse

Break Free - Emotional Self Help, Emotional Healing, and Emotional Health

© **Copyright 2015 - All rights reserved.**

In no way is it legal to reproduce, duplicate, or transmit any part of this document in either electronic means or in printed format. Recording of this publication is strictly prohibited and any storage of this document is not allowed unless with written permission from the publisher. All rights reserved.

The information provided herein is stated to be truthful and consistent, in that any liability, in terms of inattention or otherwise, by any usage or abuse of any policies, processes, or directions contained within is the solitary and utter responsibility of the recipient reader. Under no circumstances will any legal responsibility or blame be held against the publisher for any reparation, damages, or monetary loss due to the information herein, either directly or indirectly.
Respective authors own all copyrights not held by the publisher.

Legal Notice:
This book is copyright protected. This is only for personal use. You cannot amend, distribute, sell, use, quote or paraphrase any part or the content within this book without the consent of the author or copyright owner. Legal action will be pursued if this is breached.

Disclaimer Notice:
Please note the information contained within this document is for educational and entertainment purposes only. Every attempt has been made to provide accurate, up to date and reliable complete information. No warranties of any kind are expressed or implied. Readers acknowledge that the author is not engaging in the rendering of legal, financial, medical or professional advice.
By reading this document, the reader agrees that under no circumstances are we responsible for any losses, direct or indirect, which are incurred as a result of the use of information contained within this document, including, but not limited to, —errors, omissions, or inaccuracies.

Table of Contents

Introduction 5

Chapter 1: The Different Types of Emotional Abuse 8

    Verbal abuse 9

    Needy expectations 10

    'I know best' abuse 11

    Drama Queen (or King!) 12

    Denial and withdrawal 13

Chapter 2: Understanding Why Emotional Abuse Happens 17

    Family history 17

    Temperament 18

    Addictive personalities 19

    Retaliation against emotional abuse at work 20

Chapter 3: Fighting Back Against Emotional Abuse 24

    Set behavioral boundaries 24

    Be confident 26

    Relax 27

    Confide in a friend 27

Chapter 4 – Dealing With The Emotional Controller 29

Chapter 5 – Emotional Abuse in Blended Families 34

Chapter 6 – Emotional Abuse to Elders **39**
    Taking control 40
    Eldercare Abuse 41
    What family members can do to help an abused elderly person 42

Chapter 7 – Emotional Abuse in the Workplace 45
    What kind of emotional abuse happens in the workplace? 45
    Rebuilding your life after emotional abuse at work 49

Chapter 8 – Emotional Abuse By Peers 50

Chapter 9: Recovering From Emotional Abuse 55
    Bury the past 57
    Repair your self-esteem 58
    Give yourself time to heal and evaluate 59
    Enjoy yourself! 59

Conclusion 61

Introduction

What is emotional abuse? Basically it is a form of abuse that is not physical in nature. Abuse is defined as controlling behavior designed to coerce, humiliate and intimidate. When that abuse is physical, it is accompanied by violence of one degree or another. When it comes to emotional abuse, the violence comes from words or disapproving or critical behavior. Whoever said that words could never hurt you had it spectacularly wrong, because in the right hands, words can be lethal weapons, and every bit as dangerous and as harmful as knives and guns.

Emotional abuse exists primarily in relationships, because to be a victim of emotional abuse, there has to be an existing closeness. Usually this closeness involves intimate partners, but it can also occur between siblings, friends and even colleagues.

It is worrying because it can impact on self-worth, self-esteem, and confidence – all those things you need to make your way in the world. Even worse, you feel that it's your entire fault, and that you're trapped in your relationship because nobody else will want you. The truth of the matter is that none of this is your fault – you have done nothing wrong whatsoever.

There are many different kinds of emotional abuse – also called psychological or mental abuse. This book will examine the various kinds of emotional abuse and help you to come to terms with what is happening and escape the destructive cycle that is emotional abuse. You can escape, you can heal yourself and you can rebuild your life. Yes – you really can!

It's important for you to have a better understanding because, until you do, you can't tackle the problem. You may not even be aware of it happening. All that you know is that your life is unhappy, that you have problems with thinking of yourself as valuable and that your esteem has been eroded. This book will help you to understand the process that goes behind emotional abuse so that you can recognize what people are doing to you and be better armed to stop the abuse and move on. Until you gain an understanding of abuse of this nature, you will allow it to continue to hamper your life. Why? Because without knowing how to stem it or even what causes it, you are not in a position to do anything to help yourself.

Abusive relationships happen from childhood right through to old age because people put themselves into positions where they lose choice. The old lady, abused by her own children who use her for her money may have nowhere else to go and think that she has no alternative but to accept emotional abuse. The child who is degraded on a regular basis into thinking that he/she has no value may equally think there is no element of choice that can help. There is. The problem is that when emotional abuse happens, the subject of that abuse doesn't always look clearly at the situation and may be influenced by their abuser.

Often children emotionally abused by parents will submit to that abuse because they feel that their parents must be right. Adults must know what they are saying and have more experience than children do. They also have more power. A teacher who emotionally bullies a child within his class because of personal issues is just as guilty as a parent if the child is put into a state of feeling inadequate as a consequence of the behavior of the teacher toward that child.

Yet this goes largely unnoticed by anyone else. That's the abuser's way of dealing with their power over the abused.

The husband who taunts his wife because she doesn't meet with his approval may be tearing down all her defenses so that she feels inadequate and useless. It's a really vicious kind of abuse because it's so covert, but nonetheless it is very real indeed. The wife may equally emotionally abuse her husband. His role is the hunter and the provider. She may mock his ability to provide. She may have power over him that makes him feel his life isn't worth anything.

The point is that you need to recognize that abuse before you are able to address it. This book covers all different angles in an attempt to help you to make sense of the abuse that you may be suffering and to do something concrete to step out of the cycle of emotional abuse.

The way to judge whether you need the book or whether it will be of any help to you is to look at your life. Is it unhappy? Do others make you feel like you have less value than you should have? Are you pushed into doing things you don't want to do? Are you receiving snide comments that really do hurt you inside? Do you have issues with mixing with people because of your lack of trust in life? This book shows you how to recognize this type of abuse and stem it.

It can make all the difference in the world to your life once you do. The emotional healing that you go through puts you back onto strong roots so that you never allow emotional abuse again, but are stronger and more able to recognize its potential, thus befriending those that merit your friendship, rather than those who may add to your uncertainty and unhappiness.

Chapter 1: The Different Types of Emotional Abuse

Physical abuse is pretty straightforward really. You get bashed with something, stabbed with something or slapped or thrown about. Emotional abuse, however, is something much more complex, because the mind is more complex than the body. You can see the marks and scars of physical abuse, but with emotional abuse, the scars are hidden inside you. However, that doesn't mean they aren't there – just that you can't see them. And emotional scars can take much longer to heal – if they ever heal at all.

Emotional abuse is also more difficult to identify, because it consists of mind games in action, and unless you are a psychologist or an emotional abuser yourself, you may have a problem with recognizing emotional abuse. Often, it's just a vague feeling – usually felt by someone else rather than the victim – that something 'isn't quite right' in a relationship. That's because emotional abusers are cunning and subtle. They can put on a benevolent face for the world, but behind closed doors, it's completely different. It is here, within the confines of a relationship between two people that they inflict their harm. It doesn't matter whether the relationship is a romantic one or simply two people that know each other – all relationships are open to emotional abuse. If something that another person does or says fills you with some kind of horror inside that makes you uncomfortable on a regular basis, then it's likely to be emotionally abusive.

These, then, are some of the different types of emotional abuse. If you feel that you or someone close to you is being subjected to something similar, it's time to get help.

Verbal abuse

This is probably the kind of emotional abuse most people are familiar with. The saying that 'Sticks and stones may break my bones but words can never hurt me' is way off the mark, because words can and do hurt, especially when there are witnesses to those words. Even when there are not, behind closed doors, the things that are said with the intention of hurting or damaging someone's psyche are emotional abuse.

Nobody is perfect, but some people seem to take great pleasure in magnifying the imperfections of others out of all proportion. Constructive criticism it is not – its just criticism, and it's negative and almost always unwarranted. It may include name-calling, shouting, sarcasm, blame, and humiliation. And if someone comes to the defense of the victim, it just makes things worse, because the abuser believes that they are right, and that anyone who disagrees is obviously in league with the victim or in love with them. While they may appear to back down in front of others, once the abuser is alone with the victim the process is intensified.

This form of emotional abuse often stems from feelings of inadequacy or jealousy on the part of the abuser. Although the criticism is not justified, it serves to erode the confidence and self-esteem of the victim, to the extent that they come to believe that the criticism is justified. Kids at school are particular astute in this kind of abuse, though they are not the only ones. People who hide behind the guise of a friend may actually do this to someone in an attempt to belittle someone so that they look better than the person being abused. Belittling someone who has a handicap and making them feel worse about their handicap than they already do is cruel, though it forms part of what is known as mental abuse.

Needy expectations

Sometimes, however much attention someone gets, it's never enough. You go out one day a month with friends for lunch, and according to your significant other, 'You're never at home.' He – or she – will go on about it for days or even weeks beforehand, and carry on about it for days or weeks after the event, destroying any enjoyment you might have obtained from meeting up with friends for good food and even better company. It's a jealousy thing. Jealousy is extremely negative and shows a real lack of confidence, but it's worse for the person who is abused by being forced to change what they do to fit in with the ideology of someone else. "You don't love me. If you loved me, you wouldn't need other friendships," may be the kind of statement that a needy person would use almost as an emotional blackmail. If the subject of that blackmail doesn't respond in the way that is required, the blackmail becomes even more obvious until they either leave the relationship or succumb to the behavior of that needy partner, hoping that things will change.

They say that no man is an island, but your man – and it's usually a man – wants you to spend all your time with him, to the exclusion of all others. Even if you do, it's still not going to be enough, because you'll be criticized, and you'll hear "'I bet you'd rather be out with your friends than here with me." The tragedy of this situation is that this is a self-fulfilling prophecy, because after a while, you will feel that you'd rather be with anyone else than your partner. Thus, it's self-defeating, serves no purpose and makes both of you feel worse about your situation.

'I know best' abuse

This is controlling behavior of the worst kind. Initially, it may be disguised as attempts to help and to give advice, but the giveaway comes when you don't act on that advice. In effect, this is along the lines of a parent-child relationship, rather than a meeting of equals. There's the insistence that you 'Do as I say, or else.' No matter how the person concerned may try to dress it up as advice, problem solving, analysis or whatever, it's emotional abuse.

Essentially, your partner is emphasizing his or her superiority by questioning your judgment on the slightest pretext. That kind of continual criticism undermines your confidence and self-belief to the point where you continually question your own judgment. Eventually, you just stop making decisions, because you have no faith in yourself, and even then, the criticism continues. With emotional abuse, there is never a place called 'Stop!' This is the kind of behavior demonstrated by a controller. That person feels that he/she has the right to control the relationship and will not rest until their demands are met. They may criticize the way that a partner dresses. They may belittle their partner in front of others and they may flirt to make their partner feel like there's not much alternative to doing as they are demanded. The subject of this kind of abuse will actually fear for the end of the relationship although an end to the relationship may actually give them more freedom. The problem is that their confidence is eroded to such an extent that they have no idea they can manage on their own.

Friends may try to deter the abused from staying within the relationship, but the problem is that the self-esteem is so eroded that listening to sensible advice is harder for them and causes them even more conflict, thinking that they must be a bad person to think negative things about the partner they have.

Drama Queen (or King!)

This form of emotional abuse is the enemy of tranquility. Basically, one partner is always starting arguments, or making mountains out of molehills. It's as if they thrive on an atmosphere of constant chaos. This type of behavior is totally unpredictable, and results in the victim being in a constant state of walking on eggshells. They are unable to enjoy anything or relax fully, because they never know when the next explosion is coming.

Living with a Drama Queen or King is perpetually stressful, and eventually it will impact on the victim's health. This is one form of emotional abuse there is no respite from, since there is always the expectation of an argument or some sort of drama. When it doesn't materialize, there is no sense of relief – just an increased feeling of dread because the abused partner knows that sooner or later it will happen, and the longer it goes without an episode, the more stressed the partner will become.

A man and woman relationship is not the only kind that suffers from this. Friendships can also be like this where there is always some kind of dilemma pushed onto the abused making the abused feel that they are doing something wrong. It also exists in parent child relationships. Have you ever seen the mom who gives the good imitation of heart problems whenever the child threatens leaving home? The abused in this case is not the mom. It's the child who is forced by obligation to stay and home and have no life at all for fear of anything happening to the parent.

Denial and withdrawal

Denial and withdrawal are two sides of the same emotional abuse coin. Denial happens when the abuser calls your own perceptions of events into question. Picture the scene. After a particularly distressing episode you are naturally quiet, even miserable. Your partner asks why, so you explain to him or her. Their response is, 'I didn't say that – I would never speak to you like that/ call you that name.' Or it may be the more subtle 'You have the wrong idea there, honey. That's not what I meant at all.' It's usually followed by something like 'How could you even think I would treat you like that? I love you too much to behave in such a way.'

Your partner may also trivialize your reactions, accusing you of exaggerating or blowing their behavior out of proportion, or suggesting that the way you responded shows that you're the one with the problem. They may even say, 'You should know by now that I don't mean it.' The thing is – they do mean it. It's all intended to undermine your self-confidence and make you question your belief in your own judgment and instincts.

What happens here is that the blame is neatly switched to your shoulders. Your partner is the one acting hurt, and it's your fault. Except you know it isn't, and you know what was said and done. However your partner's distorted view of events, if repeated often enough, will have you questioning your own perceptions, and maybe even your sanity. And that can lead to more abuse, because you're testing out your perceptions and maybe allowing stuff to go on for longer, just so you know exactly what's happening. It won't make any difference though – your partner will still deny that he or she has a problem, and place the blame on your paranoia.

Withdrawal is an extension of this, because your partner denies you the chance to talk things through by going silent on you after an argument, or when he's upset by something you did, or something he thinks you did. The silent treatment can go on for hours, days or even weeks, and it's very damaging, as it creates tension and conflict. During the silent period, each of you is becoming more agitated, which will inevitably result in further unpleasantness when the silence is broken.

Each of the described behaviors is a form of emotional abuse, and you should not have to tolerate it. However, you probably will, because you feel increasingly isolated, and as if it is you that has the problem, not your abuser. That's because emotional abuse erodes your self-confidence and self-worth, to the point where you believe that you don't deserve to be happy, and if you end your relationship, you will spend the rest of your life alone.

One way to get out of this rut of despair is to understand why emotional abuse happens, and why it is directed at you. Then you can look for a way to either end the abuse escape from the negative relationship you have been trapped in for so long. Remember – it's not you who has the problem, and it's not you who needs to change. Imagine the scenario. A husband is unfaithful to his wife and yet it's her that feels bad and feels guilty and small when he leaves her. Emotions play a great big part in emotional abuse and the emotional abuser knows it. However, you do need to change the destructive cycle of behavior that has controlled and blighted your life for so long. You need to change your own perspective and your approach to this form of abuse to stop the cycle.

Adult Child emotional abuse

One may imagine that adults would know better than to abuse children, but when you see abuse on the news, it isn't just sexual abuse that causes harm to kids. Emotional abuse can devastate their lives and follow them well into adulthood. A parent is supposed to nurture a child and make that child feel that he/she has a place in this world that is valued. Instead, parents hold an emotional gun to children's heads and use emotional abuse to belittle them or to make them feel bad about their choices even when those choices are valid. Parents who do this may make a child feel that the child has no value. The child may become very withdrawn as a consequence of this abuse but it isn't just parents who are guilty. Teachers can use this kind of abuse to belittle a child that the teacher doesn't like. You may think that a little far-fetched but ask kids because although I am a grown up now, I still bear the scars of emotional abuse of a math teacher who made me so afraid of getting answers wrong that I hid for hours in the school toilets when it was time for math.

How does that affect me now? I still remember that feeling of being afraid and will never allow myself to go there again. It took me years to feel confidence and to be able to accept that being good at math didn't measure how good I was as a person. I had a much similar experience with a gym teacher because I was overweight and not prone to be good at sports. Those lessons were hard ones for a child. I was mentally abused by the teacher and mocked for not being as developed as other kids. That's a very cruel kind of abuse to inflict on a child who is just learning all about development and the issues that face them as they go through puberty. That hollow and cold feeling inside that makes you want to hide away still affects me sometimes when cruel things happen which is part of the reason this book was written. No one should have to suffer that kind of behavior, but yet every day, people do.

Knowledge is power, and if you know why your partner is an emotional abuser that knowledge can help you to mitigate the situation.

Chapter 2: Understanding Why Emotional Abuse Happens

Emotional abusers are not born with a rogue gene that compels them to verbally abuse, belittle and control others. They learn to behave that way because of events in their lives that they haven't been able to cope with in a healthy way. This can be down to upbringing, social and cultural influences or underlying psychological conditions. Abusers don't carry a government health warning for all to see, and they can be difficult to identify. So you need a few clues to help you to identify emotional abusers, and also understand where their behavior is coming from.

Family history

While not all people who come from abusive family relationships go on to abuse – either emotionally or physically – people who grow up in an emotionally abusive home are more likely to become abusers themselves. Children learn from their parents, and if those parents are controlling and abusive, there's a good chance they will replicate that behavior in their own adult relationships. People gravitate to the familiar, and feel more comfortable with it. Having read several stories of emotional abuse, the pattern seems a very familiar one. In one book, the abuser was asked why he treated his wife in a certain way. His reply was "There's nothing wrong with my behavior. My father acted in the same way as I do." He was convinced that it was the behavior of his wife that was at fault and that normal people abused each other in this way and it meant nothing unusual at all. In fact, his wife learned to gain strength and eventually escaped the marriage before it killed her. The abuse was as serious as that and the problems that she suffered to her self-esteem lasted for years after having left. Of course, it's possible to move on from abuse, but you need to find strength inside you to do that. It also takes a bit of time to build yourself back up into the whole person that you always were, but without the presence of constant abuse, it's easier.

If your partner has grown up in an emotionally abusive home, he – or she – is likely to replicate that behavior, because it's all they understand. Maybe they've seen one parent abuse the other, or the parents abuse themselves or other children. To them, it's normal – it's what everyone does. Except of course, it isn't.

If a partner has been brought up in a controlling household, where they have had no opportunity to make their own decisions and mistakes, they have had no opportunity to grow emotionally. The only thing they know is control, and this is what they do best. What most people don't put into the picture is that controllers take delight in abusing those who are weaker and more prone to do as they are bid.

Temperament

Some people naturally have a shorter fuse than others. It doesn't take a lot to push their buttons. They are impatient, and they may have anger management issues. Perhaps they are perfectionists, and anything short of perfection is failure. Their expectations are set at such a high level that nobody can reasonably expect to match them, and when their partner inevitably falls short, they can't deal with it. These people may also abuse in the workplace making people feel that they are not good enough to be working there and consequently making life hell for the abused during the hours of work.

Basically, the abuser's expectations are unrealistic, although he or she may not think so. Whatever you do is not good enough. The type of people who are temperamentally predisposed to emotional abuse are also likely to be suspicious and jealous, whether they have reason to be or not.

Addictive personalities

People with addictive personalities are more likely to be emotional abusers, mainly due to the fact that substance abuse can cause mood swings. Behavior that is acceptable when they are sober or clean is a problem when they are drunk or high. You never know where you are, because they never know where they are.

If someone has an addiction – whether it's smoking, drinking, drugs, gambling or something else – their self-esteem is low, because deep down, they despise themselves because they are in the grip of addiction. Their response to this is to criticize the behavior of those closest to them, effectively transferring the blame. The fact that you are not addictive goes against you.

You would have to live with an addictive personality to see how this kind of abuse happens. When things go wrong, it is never their fault. They cast the blame toward the nearest person and they control the situation by always bringing that person down. A married person can begin to feel like an outsider and those who are addicted can make them feel inferior because they simply don't get addiction or have any clue about it. They may even refer to past relationships and make a partner feel like the marriage was a mistake if the non-addicted partner tries to help in any way. Thus, it can take away the power of the partner and psychologically damage their confidence.

Retaliation against emotional abuse at work

Sometimes, emotional abuse is a response by someone who is being emotionally abused and wants to reclaim control. More often than not, the way they choose to do this is to become controlling at home, because they see their partner as a soft target. They don't feel they can hit out at their boss or colleague – maybe because they are afraid of repercussions. They may feel they are at risk of losing professional respect, or their job, and with it financial security. So they put up with the abuse at work, and then go home and take it out on their nearest and dearest.

If you try to talk about it, they will deny there is a problem, because they don't want to get into that sort of thing. They won't admit there's a problem, because they don't see their reaction as a problem. It seems a perfectly logical response.

People become emotional abusers for a number of reasons. If you can identify the source of the problem, it can help you to escape from the cycle of emotional abuse. If nothing else, knowing why your partner behaves as he or she does will at least prove to you that the problem is not yours, and that you are not deserving of emotional abuse. Recapping all of the reasons gives you a quick overview of why people do this and what they gain from it. This may help you to identify if you are being emotionally abused.

Family History of abuse

This is the number one reason why people emotionally abuse and if there is a family history, this needs to be addressed

Inadequacy

In this case, the abuser hides the inadequacy by bullying. In this case, it's necessary to look deeper into the reasons.

The controller

If you feel unreasonably controlled, you may need help to break the cycle

The stormy temperamental abuser

This will also show in the pattern of behavior and is one of the easiest types to identify

The addicted or Inadequate

These abusers also show signs of their addiction or their inadequacy which may give clues

The frustrated worker

If anger seems to follow illogically after work, perhaps your partner is having problems within the work environment and knows of no other way to find release.

There is no excuse for anyone treating you in a way that makes you feel uncomfortable. If people who call themselves friends do this to you, you can count them among your toxic friends and try to distance yourself from them. It's harder to get away from family members who use emotional abuse to make you feel bad, but you can seek help. There are helplines for people who are experiencing this kind of abuse and the centers are trained to be able to recognize whether this is really abuse or whether it is simply a misunderstanding. If you feel at risk and want someone to talk to, then you can talk to people on the helplines because they are independent of your situation and can give you neutral advice and help.

The number for children is 1-800-4-A-CHILD (2-24453)

The number for adults in relationships that are abusive is 1.800.799.SAFE (7233)

These are not just lines for violent abuse. It is well known that the emotional abuse that people suffer can be just as hard for them to deal with. Children are able to talk about problems with adults that are affecting them and the experts are able to offer good advice to help them to move forward in a positive way.

If you have been able to recognize that you are being abused, then it's time to realize that unless some action is taken, it's unlikely that your abuser will stop abusing you. In the coming chapters, we will cover ways in which you can minimize the damage in certain cases and referring to this chapter occasionally when you feel that someone is affecting you adversely may also remind you that it's not acceptable to abuse someone emotionally or in a violent way. Never think that you deserve it as no one ever does. Human beings have to learn to cohabit without taking advantage of the emotions of other parties within the home because once these emotions are played with; it really can make life very miserable indeed.

If you feel that your relationship is abusive, it's time to assess the situation and to start to keep a log of situations where you feel that emotional abuse has been used to make you feel bad or worse, which is eroding your self-confidence. Sometimes it pays to write down events that happen and try to make sense of them but always do this in private and make sure that you don't keep the notes because if an abuser finds them, it may give them even more fuel to abuse you.

The reason this helps is because you can see things more clearly and it may satisfy you that you didn't do anything wrong and help you to keep your morale intact. I once wrote down a whole conversation and then went over it and found out what triggered the abuse and that was a really good exercise because it helped to stop the same abuse from happening again. This took place in the workplace and I had offered to help someone because my own workload was fairly light and I thought that theirs looked rather cumbersome. Reading back through the conversation, I was able to see it from their point of view and what it looked like was that I was suggesting that perhaps I was better than that other person was, though it was not intended. The abuse the followed went on for a while and I was able to stem it by seeing my own part in it and explaining that the only reason I had asked to help was because I had nothing really satisfying to do. I also apologized for any misunderstanding.

Chapter 3: Fighting Back Against Emotional Abuse

You may feel like you are trapped in your emotionally abusive relationship, but you're not – although it may not be easy to escape the abuse. Before you can do that though, you have to recognize that it is not your fault, and that you do not deserve to be treated this way. Understanding why your partner behaves as he or she does is the first step to breaking free of the destructive cycle of abuse.

Set behavioral boundaries

It may sound obvious, but the first thing to do is make it clear to your partner that you are not prepared to tolerate emotional abuse. When it starts, say 'I will not tolerate this from you,' and try to stay calm and quiet. If it continues, repeat that you will not listen to insults and abuse. If it still carries on, remove yourself from the scene. Either go to another room, or leave the house, but don't stay there and take the abuse. Your partner is only able to keep it up if you stay there and take it. If you remove yourself, that's the end of it for the time being.

There is something that you need to know about emotional abuse. It can only hurt you if you allow it to. If you know that the abuse is coming from your partner's inadequacy at dealing with life, then trying to shout back or trying to gain control may not be the best move. It's far more beneficial to tell your partner that the behavior is unacceptable and to stay calm and distance yourself from him/her until both of you have had a chance to calm down.

It's difficult to remain calm and not get upset in the face of a verbal onslaught, but if your reaction is not the expected one, you are not reinforcing and validating their behavior. If you can do this every time the verbal abuse starts, you should find that the intervals between episodes get longer and longer. You need to be consistent though – each time the abuse starts, adopt the 'two strikes, then I'm out of here' approach.

If your partner is not getting the reaction he wants – that is, you being visibly upset and begging him to stop – he just may decide it's not worth it. If the abuse has been going on for a long time, it may take a while to get to this stage. And you have to be ready to face the fact that it may never stop if the behavior is deeply ingrained. However, if you are consistent and give it a fair chance, this method of dealing with verbal abuse can be very effective.

Mirroring

You may not know this system of dealing with unreasonable behavior. If you listen to what your abuser is saying to you and mirror it back, often the abuser sees what they have said as being unreasonable. Words are often shouted in anger. Manipulators, however, may be more difficult to deal with because they have planned their abuse. They know exactly what they are doing to you and mirroring will not work in this case. I will give you an example.

"You are a pathetic bitch! Have you ever seen how pathetic you are?"

Your reply to this would probably be emotional and you may have shouted in the past in response to an insult of this nature. However, when you use mirroring, you remain very calm and collected. Your reply wouldn't be the response that they will be expecting. They expect tears; they want to hurt you in that moment although that's not to say that they do it intentionally. Perhaps they are displacing anger and you are the nearest target.

"Thank you for pointing that out. I can't say that I noticed that I was pathetic."

It sounds too easy to be true, but the first time that you reply in this manner, you may get an angry retort, but you are mirroring what they said. They told you that you are pathetic. You are calm. You don't allow emotions to make you appear pathetic as they are suggesting that you are. You thank them for their input and repeat the word "pathetic" because an abuser may not actually have thought about what they are saying and may regret having said it.

The problem with abusers is that they expect you to respond by showing them just how pathetic you are. They expect tears, they expect you to show emotional instability and it validates what they have said to you. If you don't give them that validation, then they get no satisfaction from trying to make you feel small, and thus will have to back off because their comments are not working.

Be confident

Emotional abuse robs you of your confidence and self-worth. In order to stop the abuse, you need to regain that lost ground. If you can't be confident, fake it until you make it. When the abuse starts, look your partner in the eye, even laugh, and tell them to stop being ridiculous. Don't cower in a corner or hang your head – hold your chin up and challenge the behavior.

Emotional abusers are like schoolyard bullies – they don't like it when someone stands up to them, and more likely than not, they will back down when challenged. Even if they don't, keep acting confident, and when they become abusive, tell them to stop. Tell them you are entitled to be treated with respect, and you will not respond to disrespectful talk or behavior. And mean it! Empty threats gain no sort of advantage.

Relax

You need to make a conscious effort to come out of the state of perpetual tension and anticipation where you are always waiting for the next episode of emotional abuse. Try some relaxation techniques such as deep breathing or meditation. Practice consciously relaxing: physically and mentally. Yoga may help with this too.

You also need to get away from the scene of the crime, as it were. Meet up with friends, or just go for a walk in the fresh air. Bury that feeling of being trapped by getting out, and relaxing your mind, so you are not always on guard, waiting for the next explosion. If you are relaxed when it happens, you are in a better starting point to change your reaction to the abuse. You can be calm and considered, and just walk away, or state that you will not put up with such behavior. If you can change your response, you are taking steps to changing the abusive behavior. Being able to effectively relax between episodes will help a lot.

Confide in a friend

There's an old saying that 'A problem shared is a problem halved,' and like many old sayings, there's a lot of truth in it. The simple fact of talking to someone who knows you well and can reassure you that you do not have a problem, and that the abuse is not your fault, can help to make you feel a whole lot better. Talking about it also helps you to see your partner's behavior for what it really is – abuse.

It's easy to fool yourself that maybe you're reading too much into it, and that it isn't as bad as you think. You may even manage to convince yourself that you are in some way responsible for your treatment. However, when you share what's happening with someone else, it becomes clearer in your own mind, and you also have the benefit of an outside perspective on it all. Once your fears are spoken, they are not so threatening or intimidating, and once your testimony of your treatment is 'out there,' things won't seem so hopeless, and you won't feel so helpless.

These strategies, either singly or combined, can help you to mitigate the effects of emotional abuse and help you to live a more relaxed and happy life. You cannot easily change the behavior of an emotional abuser, but you can change the way you react to abuse. If your partner is not getting the response he or she hoped for and expected, it may cause them to rethink their behavior.

Chapter 4 – Dealing With The Emotional Controller

When you find yourself in a situation where abuse is happening on a regular basis, you may find that this started a long time ago. Emotional controllers are not nice people. They may appear to be everything that you need, but that's only because they have fed you that line so often that you believe you cannot live without them. These are the types of people who make you go through hoops to get anything that you want in your life and will always make you think of their comforts first. They will also have good reasons why you can't do the things that you want to do. You may hear retorts like:

"Is that all you think of our marriage?"

Or

"I thought you had more respect for me than that."

Whatever the comment, it will make you back off because they are very skilled at doing this. The emotional controller will throw all of the rules of decent relationships out of the book and will give you the impression that they are actually doing you a huge service being in your life. You may hear them saying that you have a lot to be thankful for and making you feel that you were unreasonable to demand something that they don't want you to do. These kinds of controllers are more common than you may imagine. It may start with subtle comments, but once you start to lose your confidence, you will find that the level of their control over you escalates. You are afraid to be seen with friends. You only phone people when your partner is not there and they may even keep you from seeing family members, making you choose between your partner and the people you should be naturally inclined to keep in touch with.

Where this kind of abuse comes from

This abuse comes from an underlying insecurity on the part of your partner, but don't be too quick to be empathetic. They are so accustomed to treating you in this manner that it's unlikely that they will acknowledge that any part of the emotional abuse is caused by their past or events within it that took away that element of security. These are not people who are shy and nervous. They are people who are determined and are unlikely to change the way that they treat you unless you take action to stop what is happening. If you object to the way that they talk to you, you are likely to make the situation worse. They will find more ways to hurt you. It seems to be the only thing that they have control over and if you try taking that control away, you place them in a position where they up the ante and treat you in an even worse way.

There is another way of dealing with people like this. If you have been with the same partner for many years, and love that partner, it's not going to be easy to break away and you may not even want to. You won't stop the abuse by simply becoming submissive. The way to do this is to gradually try to befriend them, to talk about things that matter and to show them that you need them. It's almost as if there is an element of fear within them that doesn't let them treat you in a normal way. I knew one girl who discovered how to stop emotional abuse by building up trust. She shared everything with her guy because it was her way of letting him know that she loved him. She told him about her dreams and disappointments, knowing that it was disappointments within his life that were making him react in the way that he was reacting. It took a lot of time, a lot of effort and a lot of trust on her part to keep up the façade that he wasn't hurting her anymore and that she could totally relate to the way he felt by demonstrating the same experience in her life. Had she criticized or even suggested that any of this negativity came from him, she would not have achieved the same result. However, patience and understanding where the emotional abuse was coming from helped her to stage her understanding in such a way that it related to her flaws rather than his. It was almost like mirror imaging, but without the person at fault being the emotional abuser.

The problem with an emotional abuser is that when they start this kind of abuse, they don't intend to hurt. It gets to be a habit as it makes them feel in control of their lives whereby in the past or in some circumstances of the past, they lost that control. Typical beginnings of emotional abuse of this nature is when a partner is in some way restrictive or starts to show a pattern of behavior where they want to have things their way and will emotionally blackmail you into letting that happen. They may not know where this comes from, but if you give into it, you give them more power and more confidence that they can continue to treat you in this manner.

You may think that emotional controllers are just a normal thing in a relationship, but if you do think like this, then you probably got into the relationship at a time when your self-esteem was already low. Controllers tend to look for weak people to choose as a partner and you may need to strengthen your approach to life and become more proactive. Taking classes in being assertive may help you, even if you give the impression to your partner that you are merely taking classes that are related to your work. If you give them the impression that you are doing this because of them, it's likely that objections will come in the way of heightened abuse.

The emotional controller will not be accustomed to getting denied whatever it is that they request. However, with a little gained confidence, you need to start to show them that you want to have some joy out of life and are not prepared to let them stop you from doing things that are important to you. The biggest threat to them is that you will leave and they believe that their emotional control is what keeps you in the relationship. If you can gradually work it into your rapport that all of the things you do make you happier and in consequence will make the relationship stronger, you will get less resistance.

One person that I knew that remained in an emotionally abusive relationship was convinced that she was in the wrong and continued to live under her husband's threat for over 40 years. When her husband died of a heart attack, she was very slow at finding her feet again, because he had never let her do anything. She couldn't drive although she had always wanted lessons. Thus, she was unable to get from A to B until she saw that it was senseless not having a driving license and living in an isolated country location. She was always told that she was useless at organization and yet she noticed that when she was on her own, her organization ability was astounding. He had made her feel worthless and it took a long time to be able to stand on her own two feet, although when she did, she admitted to being a very happy person because she hadn't realized the impact of the emotional abuse when he was alive. She had merely thought herself incapable and had self-esteem issues that were made even worse because she had little contact with anyone who gave her any reason to think she was valuable. Her husband saw to that.

Emotional control isn't fair. If you find any element of this happening in your relationship, you need to stem it by calm talk and perhaps a little reassurance, and by making sure that your partner knows that your love is solid but that your life should not be one that imposes restrictions. Your partner may not be aware that instead of making himself feel secure, he may be endangering the relationship by trying to take control.

Chapter 5 – Emotional Abuse in Blended Families

You may have bought this book because you find yourself in a situation where an adult is emotionally abusing you within your blended family. Perhaps you are a child who is being treated badly by a stepparent. It is quite common for children to be made the victims when blended families get together. The problem may be that the stepmother or stepfather may resent you because you are not their child. They may show emotional abuse in very subtle ways that your birth parent is not noticing. Here are some of the ways that this is shown toward a child by a stepparent:

The stepparent treats you as if you were inferior to his/her own children

You get less emotional support from the stepparent

You are criticized when your birth parent is not around

Your stepparent mocks you and makes you feel unimportant

Other ways that a child can be made to feel bad within a blended family is when the natural parent turns against the child because he/she feels that the child is a reminder of the old broken relationship. Typical comments may be:

"You are every bit as disappointing as your father!"

"You should go and live with your mother!"

"I wish you'd never been born."

The reason this is happening is because your parent's new partner may be putting pressure on your parent concerning your role in the home. It isn't fair to do this to children but it does happen and you need to be prepared to seek help if you find this happening to you. Children are often afraid to talk about things such as this because they feel that it's disloyal to a parent or stepparent. However, helplines are available for children and they can also seek help at school if they are finding the situation too stressful.

The symptoms of emotional abuse toward a child may have already become apparent to teachers. Your grades may be going down, you may find problems in concentration levels and may even find that you don't make friends easily because you are too troubled and afraid. If you do find yourself in this predicament, you really do need to seek help. If, on the other hand, it's only the stepparent who is abusing you, you need to get your natural parent in a situation where you can feel free to talk about your problems. Chances are that your parent is unaware of what is going on and may be able to change the situation by discussing this with your stepparent.

If you feel that you need psychological help, you can talk to your teachers at school and they may be able to suggest this to your parent, so that the parent is aware that something is troubling you, even though they may have no clue that it's their attitude toward you. Often, talking with someone outside the family will help you to overcome the difficulty that you have to face.

There are several types of emotional abuse that can be happening to a child and which are very negative for the child to handle alone:

Rejection – Making a child feel that he/she isn't good enough or doesn't measure up.

Ignoring – This can be equally damaging to a child who needs help but is not getting it from family members.

Using Fear or Terror – This can happen in blended families when threats are used and a child is left to live in fear. It can even happen between siblings if left unchecked.

Exploitation – This means making children do things that they don't want to do or things beyond their age capability.

If you are afraid to talk to anyone that you know about this kind of abuse but think that it applies to you, do telephone the helpline number shown in a previous chapter because they will be able to help you through those difficult times and know whether you need to be away from the adults who are treating you in this way. Don't be afraid of consequences. If you truly believe that your wellbeing is in danger, you are perfectly justified in asking for help. If indeed action is taken to put you into a healthier environment, it will not have the repercussions that you imagine because you will be protected.

If you notice this kind of abuse in children, report it because the child may feel too weakened by the abuse to make a report. Similarly if you are about to become part of a blended family, you need to use these guidelines to stop emotional abuse from happening within your new family unit. These are guidelines and each parent will make their own choices, but agreement between parents about how to deal with kids from different family backgrounds is vital.

- Parents should agree not to take sides in arguments
- Parents should agree that the same discipline applies to all kids
- Parents should straighten out any problems with kids before the wedding day
- They should also consult with kids to find out if the kids feel uneasy about anything
- Parents should remember that the children have already suffered the trauma of separation and appreciate that the kids need extra care rather than less
- Parents should put their own romance on a backburner in favor of family life

All kinds of misunderstandings can occur if a parent shows favor toward one particular child and another is emotionally made to feel less worthy. That's not a fair thing for a child who has already been through the trauma of divorce to experience. When divorce happens, the child loses the foundation of his/her life. To add more complexity to the situation in a new marriage is unfair.

A child in this situation needs to decide whether the abuse is so bad that they need to be moved out of the situation or whether it can be dealt with by talking with their natural birth parent. Parents should listen to the needs of children but sometimes they don't. In this situation, if things get too bad or out of control for the child, he/she should either ring a helpline or ask the advice of school staff who may be able to report what is happening and bring it to a close.

Children often take emotional abuse memories into adult life and they can affect how the child sees the world. It may take some time for a child to heal from this kind of abuse and the child may be withdrawn and have a lack of trust for adults because of the experience that they have undergone. Thus, authorities who deal with situations like this more and more often these days will be able to assess if the child needs to be taken away from the home situation or whether the parents need to be involved in family counseling.

If the latter is chosen, then all members of the extended family may be involved in discussions that are intended to help the family to manage their affairs without emotional abuse being allowed to continue. A specialist counselor may judge the situation and if the child is in need of further help, can usually provide it or see to it that the child gets the help needed.

Chapter 6 – Emotional Abuse to Elders

Unfortunately, elderly people are not immune to emotional abuse. Their abusers will use the fact that the elderly person is weaker and more vulnerable than the abuser and this comes in many forms, as shown below.

- The abuser makes the elderly person feel like he/she is a burden

- The abuser may make the elderly person feel like an outsider

- The abuser may threaten the elderly person with being put in a home

- The abuser may literally make the elderly person feel physically afraid

Situations such as this occur in life and they shouldn't. These are people who have given away a lot of their years to looking after and rearing children. When one parent dies, the other is left for the family to look after. In other societies, elderly people are always respected and welcomed into a family home when they reach a certain age, but unfortunately, in western society this isn't how it works.

The elderly person becomes a burden and the disruption to family life can be a real upheaval. However, it's a very unkind way to dealing with it if an elderly person is made to suffer emotional abuse because of a situation over which they have little control.

Taking control

If an elderly person feels that a child is abusing them, they need to take action. Often this won't be easy to do because self-worth will feel like it's non-existent and that makes it extremely difficult to voice an opinion. However, look at all aspects of the situation and you may decide that it would be preferable to change where you are living. If this means assisted care and you can afford it, speak to your abuser and make it clear that if you are beginning to be more trouble to them than they can manage, you are quite willing to seek alternative accommodation.

You may find that this is enough to make them think twice about continuing the abuse. They may, for example, be depending upon your contribution to the home finances and think twice about making you feel so uncomfortable. Yes, it's giving them something to think about when you have actually been investigating alternative accommodation and seeing a brochure in the post may actually confirm to them that they are pushing the emotional abuse too far and that you are not prepared to let this go on.

If you are too ill to take on your abusers, there are other alternatives open to you. Try to talk to someone about your problems and the helpline below may be of use to you. These are people who care about the elderly and who will be able to give you advice on what's available in your area in the way of help to overcome problems of this nature. There may be counseling available. There may also be day care which gets you out of the hostile environment and there may indeed be elder care residences which allow you your independence and which are affordable alternatives. Life doesn't have to grind to a halt just because you are getting older and you certainly don't have to put up with abuse. Many elder care establishments give residents their own personal space with cooking facilities and a warden who can be called when any problems occur on the health front. These may be more enjoyable than living with relatives who don't want you there, or who are using your money without actually bothering to care about you. In places such as this, you can start a good social life, mix with others in the same predicament and make new friends.

Eldercare Abuse

If you find that the abuse is happening within a facility where you are supposed to be cared for, then you should make sure that your voice is heard. The kinds of abuse that can happen within a care facility with uncaring staff are these:

- The patient feels ridiculed by a particular member of staff
- Using the elderly person as a scapegoat when things are not done correctly
- Shouting or threatening the patient
- Keeping an elderly person isolated from seeing friends and other patients
- Forcing an elderly person who enjoys their own company to mix with others
- Perpetual ignoring of the needs of the patient

If the situation is happening with one particular member of staff who is not in charge of the facility, the elderly person needs to complain to those who are in charge and be very specific about events that have brought rise to the complaint. Thus, keeping a diary of events to back up accusations is important. In an establishment that wants to keep its reputation, it is unlikely that this kind of behavior will be tolerated. The helpline number for elderly patients who are suffering abuse is shown below and can be used by them or by a family member who is concerned about a relative.

1-888-554-1010

What family members can do to help an abused elderly person

If you have an elderly relative and you suspect that they are being emotionally abused, don't be afraid to do something about it. Removal from the facility may be necessary if you don't get immediate satisfaction or if the elderly person cannot be placed within that facility away from the abuser. A responsible nursing home will get rid of staff that abuse patients. If this does not appear to be happening and you feel that an elderly relative is in danger of continued abuse, then removal may be the only option available.

If you can move that person to your home to get them into a friendlier environment, even if this is on a temporary basis, bear in mind that they will need care and assessment because the damage may already be done and they will have lost a lot of confidence.

There are specialists who deal with counseling elderly people who have been emotionally abused and it will be worth it because the psychologist can help to build up their emotional stability and help them to recover from the abuse. Sometimes, people can't do this on their own and family love and support will help, but may not be enough. If you feel that it's a lot to handle, there are day facilities that you can place your elderly relative into so that your day to day lives are not too disrupted until you manage to find a more suitable placement for the elderly person.

If you cannot afford counseling, this may be provided by the state and it is worth getting the elderly person assessed so that appropriate measures can be taken to help him/her recover from this abuse. The abuse will have left a mark and the only way forward is by believing in the elderly person and listening to their complaints, assuring them that you have done all that you can to stop the abuse from happening. In a caring environment, with adequate counseling, they can regain their confidence and this gives you time to search for a more suitable facility with a better reputation of care.

There is never any excuse of elder abuse, but it happens more often than you might imagine. The helpline given above is manned by staff that is experienced in dealing with victims of elder abuse. They will know the options available to you and will be able to take necessary action to help you to get out of the situation as quickly as possible.

Chapter 7 – Emotional Abuse in the Workplace

You may not have experienced this yourself but you may have seen people who have been treated badly within the workplace. If, however, you have found yourself in a situation where you dread going to work because of emotional abuse from a colleague, you need to take action as soon as you can so that it does not wear away your resistance and your self-esteem.

What kind of emotional abuse happens in the workplace?

Emotional abuse in the workplace can take on various guises and you may not recognize it straight away. However, if you get to the stage where you need to avoid fellow employees and go home at night dreading the next day, then you need to look to see if any of the following behavior is happening:

- You are made to look small in front of others
- You are being laden with too much work intentionally
- You are being spoken to in an inappropriate way
- You feel that your job is threatened if you say anything
- You are physically afraid of someone

There are correct channels for dealing with abuse in the workplace, though emotional abuse is harder to prove and may just make you look neurotic. If you think that you are being abused, keep a note of the events that make you feel this way so that if you need to refer to these when communicating with your Personnel staff, you will have a record. It shouldn't come to that, but it's as well to note all of the behavior that is making you feel put down and abused.

Establish if it is abuse

What you perceive to be abuse may not be. If you can confide in your immediate boss, try to make an appointment to discuss your situation. You could approach this by saying that the workplace is upsetting you and that you are not sure if you are being overly sensitive or whether the bully or the person emotionally abusing you is known for this kind of behavior and needs to be stopped. It may be that your characters clash and this can happen in the workplace, but by making your boss aware of it, he may be able to move you so that you don't have to put up with the same kind of behavior. Often people who are trying to motivate their staff will make changes of this nature so that no one feels oppressed by the workplace. It doesn't help productivity and it certainly isn't helping those who have a clash of personality. In this case, maybe the other person feels equally annoyed or upset when she/he goes home in the evening because for some reason, you two really haven't hit it off and don't see things in the same light.

If your case is justified and your boss is not prepared to take any action, you need to work out whether it's worth taking the matter further, or whether you could ask for a transfer or in fact leave the job that gives you so little satisfaction. The problem is that if you don't have your boss on your side, that's not going to help your case, so you need to decide whether to move on. Sometimes it's a healthier move to do this, rather than work in a situation where people are permitted to be so rude or manipulative.

If you think that you are being given more than your fair share of work, look through your contract and look particularly at the job description. If you are being asked to do work which falls outside the scope of your job, simply tell the person overloading you that it doesn't fall within the scope of your job.

It's a very difficult situation when you are afraid of losing your job and depend upon the money that you earn. Can you afford to make cutbacks in expenses so that a job that pays less and may suit your temperament better becomes a possibility? Sometimes, a total change of scene brings about new ideas and you can move on from emotional abuse with your pride intact and find that the new job gives you much more satisfaction than the old one did. If you are unable to move jobs, think about what's in it for the abuser.

- The abuser wants to show you his/her superiority
- The abuser wants to see you visibly upset
- The abuser wants to make you look foolish
- The abuser likes to pick on people

Most people that use emotional abuse are pretty weak. They actually gain strength from your reaction. If you end up in tears, they feel like they are stronger than you. If you try to argue back, you make them feel important enough to start an argument. If you don't react to emotional abusers, they notice that their words are doing very little and move on to abuse someone else who will show reactions.

It's very hard to show no reaction when you crying inside. No one should be subjected to this behavior in the workplace and as you spend a lot of time in the workplace every day, it's not a good thing to have to face and will eventually wear you down to such an extent that your self-esteem is gone and you don't like yourself very much. If you can merely be polite to the person who is abusing you and show no emotional reaction to their chiding, you make your position stronger. Breathe deeply. Be silent in your mind before responding and when you respond, be polite and friendly and they will know that their words have little effect on you.

The first place to try and solve something like this is with the person him/herself. Don't shake in your shoes. Don't approach the person when you feel emotional. That's a recipe for disaster. Approach when that person is not expecting it and question whether they have a problem with you. If they ask you why, you can merely state that you picked up on their vibes that they are not very happy and just wondered if you can do something to help. It sounds easy and it isn't but it is very effective. Keep your cool at all times. Offer assistance and be friendly. If that doesn't work, you still have the opportunity to talk to your boss or the personnel department or to ask for a transfer to get away from them.

Rebuilding your life after emotional abuse at work

There are several good ways forward after you have been abused. One of them is to go on an assertiveness class that shows you how to stand up for yourself and make your point clear when dealing with people. This can help you to build up your self-esteem and feel good about contact with people within the workplace. Other solutions are talking to a counselor though only if you feel this will help you. You may be left with emotional scars that will take time to heal, but by working through all of this negative thought, you will get there. Engage in things that you enjoy outside of the workplace so that you build up your positive attitude to life. You are worthy of feeling good about your life, regardless of how small that abuser made you feel.

Getting away from the abuser or changing their attitude toward you helps you to learn from the experience and never let yourself be bullied in this way again. Emotional people often feel the pressure when faced with insensitivity and rudeness and abusers won't stop just because you ask them to. If you can show an abuser that they are having little effect on your emotions, you are placing yourself in a better and much stronger position.

Chapter 8 – Emotional Abuse By Peers

Believe it or not, this can happen at any age at all. Although one may assume that this means school friends or your social circle when you are young, it also includes older people within their social circle. With the world putting such pressure on people to succeed, successful peers may actually make those who have less feel that they are lacking in some way. This kind of emotional abuse is terrible to see. The typical situations where it can occur are these:

- Older kids at school don't want to mix with the target child and tease

- Neighbors may make comments that give the impression that the target has less value

- Peers may judge someone for the way that they dress

- Peers may judge someone because they don't have the same luxuries

- Peers may use the target and emotionally blackmail them

This kind of peer pressure that amounts to emotional abuse can happen even in a ghetto where kids are not acting as "cool" as other kids. Perhaps criminals within the social circle of the victim make the victim feel that he/she isn't tough enough and can't fit into that circle any more unless the victim proves him/herself in some way. This can be very scary for a child from a deprived home who is trying his/her best to make their parents proud. It's hard for kids to resist doing wrong things when pushed around by use of this kind of emotional blackmail. If you find yourself under pressure in this way, seek adult help. There are many associations that can give you the support that you need and these may be youth associations or even the church.

You need to resist doing things that you know to be wrong and also show a brave face when peers put pressure on you. It's hard and you will find that if you level with your parents, chances are that they will give you extra strength. If you are afraid because of this emotional abuse, don't keep it a secret. It's important to talk to someone so that they can give you solid advice. Your future may be at stake and it's not worth getting yourself into big trouble just because someone else thought that you should.

Often when you take bullies like this away from their gangs or group of peers, they are pretty weak characters that only gain stature by making others afraid. They can't relate to real friendships and are certainly not doing you any favors.

In a neighbor situation, if you are suffering from emotional abuse of any sort within your social circle, it's unacceptable. Even though you may be someone who doesn't want to make waves or someone who doesn't have a lot of confidence, you have to believe that abusers will eventually break you down so that you have none at all if you let them. If you find that these people are within your social circle and are making your life miserable, learn to exclude them. Why impose negativity into your life?

The problem is that people are afraid of what others think and sometimes this gets in the way of common sense. You are no less of a person just because you dress differently to someone else. You are no less of a person because you don't wear designer label clothing.

Try to look at it this way. If everyone were judged in that way, it would be a very shallow world. Although you may wish you could afford all the things that your peers who are teasing you can afford, life isn't about what you own. It's about whom you are inside and if they rely so much upon designer labels to give them an identity, it's very sad indeed and you perhaps need to see the sad side of these people and feel sorry for them, rather than wishing you were the same as them.

Once you break away from people like this, you learn that it isn't your values that are wrong. It's theirs. If they are emotionally pulling your strings, cut the strings. You are not someone else's puppet. You are a valuable individual and you don't need to have that negative person in your life. It's easy to bail out on someone like this, although at first you may find it hard. Tell them "I'm sorry, I have other arrangements," when they ask you out. They may press you for details, but you are not obliged to explain your life to them or open yourself up for further abuse.

The problem with people such as this is that your unhappiness and your lack of measuring up makes them feel more powerful and better than you. That shows that they have lack of confidence and that the only way they can gain that confidence is by making you feel small.

When you manage to say goodbye to toxic relationships, you also begin to see things in perspective and realize it's not you that is in the wrong. It's them. From a distance, it's a lot easier to see this kind of abuse. You don't need to be in his or her set to be someone. You are already someone and once you show him or her that you don't need their emotional abuse, they will find someone else to pick on who is weaker than you and who responds to their abuse more than you do.

It's a sad fact of life that emotional abuse among peers is common. These are people that the vulnerable trust. They are supposed to be friends so their criticism is taken seriously. Instead of doing that, you need to step aside and make your own life rules instead of trying to live up to other people's expectations.

Your life isn't about designer labels. It's deeper than that and has more purpose. Walk away and find friends who accept you as you are before you let these abusers give you an inferiority complex that may make your future a total misery. You may be afraid of taking that move, but when you do, you will wonder why you didn't do that years ago. No one should be able to live your life for you or make choices for you but you.

To walk away from a relationship of this nature doesn't make you a failure. It makes you more valuable because you are showing you are not prepared to be ridiculed any more by someone you actually see as ridiculous. In the modern era, competition between peers is rife, but it shouldn't be about whether you have an iPhone or not. It should be about whether you remember how to be decent to your friends and these abusers have obviously forgotten the main rules of friendship and in the process are treating you badly because of some lack in their own lives.

Take a look around you at friends that you value and that give you an equal amount of respect. These are the peers who are setting you the right example and won't tease you or emotionally blackmail you to make themselves feel more important. That's not what good friendships are all about and it's important to realize this and to choose your friendships carefully in the future.

If you even hint that a peer is putting pressure on you or making you feel uncomfortable about whom you are, then that isn't a friend. It's an abuser. If there is no element of truth in what they say and it's shallow in nature, you will do your self-esteem more good by realizing that possessions don't define you. What's in your heart does and you have no need to let people like this have a hold over you or make you feel bad about living in the way that you can afford and the way you choose to live.

Chapter 9: Recovering From Emotional Abuse

While it can take a long time for the psychological scars of emotional abuse to heal, it is possible to enjoy life again, whether with your partner or alone. It may be that the only way to end the emotional abuse is to end the relationship, but this is something only you can decide. Here are some ideas to help you recover your love of life when the emotional abuse is over. Remember that the reason that the relationship between you and the abuser came to an end was that you needed to take control of your own destiny. Even if you managed to stay in the relationship, you still need recovery time to build your self-esteem and to rebuild the missing trust that emotional abuse takes out of the relationship.

If you are a child who has suffered emotional abuse, make sure as you grow older that you try to mix with friends who are positive in their attitudes toward life. These people are those that help you to build up your self-esteem regardless of continued abuse from relatives or people who should treat you better. I had a situation like this with a sister. What you need to do is distance yourself, as far as possible, from the abuser and when your lives touch, learn to be oblivious to what they say. The thing is that what they say doesn't figure much in your life any more so don't let it get under your skin. For years, I let my sister have this negative impact on my life, but when I stopped allowing that negative impact, she stopped using emotional abuse. She wasn't getting validation so it wasn't worth her effort. Mixing with people who are well balanced and positive will help to give you confidence and snide remarks from people who should love you and be supportive will be like water off a duck's back.

Eventually in your life, you realize that you are not who other people define you to be unless you permit them that power. I wasn't the person my sister made me feel I was. I was better than that and the positive friendships that I made told me that the weakness was hers rather than mine. There was a very good quotation that I read the other day that said something like this:

"Shouting and insults say nothing about the person who is being insulted, but they speak volumes for the person who uses this tone."

It's actually true and to this day, my sister is still the weak link in the family who cannot find happiness within her and will make others feel bad because it validates her own importance. Don't let family members do this to you. The moment you validate what they say by reacting you effectively give in to their abuse of you as if they have the right to criticize you in this negative manner. They don't have that right. Imagine yourself doing that to someone and you begin to see how sad the abuser really is and can empathize. Unfortunately empathy doesn't work well for anything except your own understanding. If you tried to sympathize and make friends with an abuser, this would accelerate the abuse.

Bury the past

Don't look back in anger or despair – look forward to the future with hope and anticipation. Once the abuse is over, let the past go, move on, and don't allow your experiences to define or influence the rest of your life. If you do, your abuser still retains control of your life. If you have problems with your ex and they will not let go of abusing you, even at a distance, then don't think twice about imposing a legal restraining order on them. The problem is that if you have children in common, it's likely that the abusive partner will try to use the kids as leverage to continue the abuse. There may be arguments over who has custody. There may be snide hints to the kids that make the kids turn against you. If you notice any of this kind of behavior, you do need to seek advice and legal recourse so that you can put an end to the cycle. In this case, do not be afraid to use the hotlines and find out what your rights are because if you continue to let your ex control your life, you cannot get beyond that abuse and start living your life again.

You control your future – remember that, and decide how your life will be from now on. If others want to talk about the past, tell them you prefer not to. If you find it difficult to let go and move on, you may benefit from counseling. Or you may find catharsis in writing about your experience, either in a journal or on a blog. Blogging has the added benefit of offering help and support to others in similar situations, so effectively something good could come out of your bad experience, which is always a positive.

The truth is, until you can let go of the past completely, you can't move forward with your life. This is why acceptance has to come first. You can let go of the past, however traumatic it may have been, but you have to really want to do so.

Repair your self-esteem

Emotional abuse can badly damage or even destroy your self-esteem, and you need to do a repair job on that as a priority. Learn to love yourself again, and value yourself as a person, because until you can value yourself, you can't expect other people to value you, and there is a risk that you may enter into another emotionally abusive relationship, or even return to the one you have escaped from. This perpetuates a destructive cycle, and it's to be avoided at all costs.

Be selfish, and spend some time on yourself. Get a great hairstyle, buy some new clothes and make up, and lose a few pounds if you need to. Concentrate on looking good, because if you look good, you feel better. Attractive, confident people attract attention from other positive people, so look your best, and if you're not quite there with the confidence, fake it until you make it. Do things that make you feel good about yourself. It isn't just about the way that you present yourself to others. If you can do things that you enjoy, you won't feel so inclined to listen to others who want to make you unhappy.

I have a trick that I use when I have self-esteem issues. I close my eyes and I imagine somewhere in this world where I was completely happy. I see the hills. I see the clouds and the sunset and I embrace it and let it make me feel at peace with who I am. Find your utopia and when people make you feel bad about yourself, find a quiet spot where you can escape to that place that you know makes you feel good about who you are.

Surround yourself with positive people, who value you as you are, and do not expect you to change to conform to their perceptions of you. Choose the people you want to associate with, and bin the negative ones, or those who keep harping on the past. You need to make the most of every moment of your life and you can't afford to let others make you this miserable.

Give yourself time to heal and evaluate

Just as physical scars take time to heal and repair, so do emotional scars. In fact emotional scars can take much longer to heal, so don't expect to feel great as soon as you leave behind your relationship. Allow yourself time to heal, and before you even think about entering into a new relationship, take the time to evaluate what you want from life and set boundaries and expectations. Otherwise, you could end up with another emotionally abusive partner.

Setting out a blueprint for future relationships is a positive thing to do, because it makes you focus on your own needs and expectations, rather than the desires of others. It's about what will make YOU happy, and when you are clear on that, you can relax and do everything you can to make your new partner happy to be with you.

Call it an emotional spring cleaning – you need to identify what was wrong in your previous relationship, and then remove it from your life so that it doesn't mess up your future. This takes time, so don't even think of looking for love again until you have your boundaries and expectations in place.

Enjoy yourself!

After coming through an emotionally abusive relationship, you will feel bruised and battered, even though there are no physical scars on show. The best way to overcome this is to consciously seek out the things you most enjoy doing. Whether it's reading a favorite book again, taking in a feel good movie, or meeting up with friends, make sure that every day contains an activity you can look forward to with pleasure and anticipation, rather than the dread of further emotional abuse.

Take up a new hobby, or join a club and meet new people. All this will help you to enjoy your new life. Spend some time enjoying being you, and other people will enjoy being around you.

It is possible to enjoy life again after leaving an emotionally abusive relationship, but you need to give yourself time to adjust to your new circumstances, and learn to savor a life free from abuse. Only then should you consider looking for love again.

Conclusion

Emotional abuse can be every bit as damaging as physical abuse. In fact, the scars can last longer, and it can take longer to identify, since there are many ways for a partner to be emotionally abusive. Often they will dress it up as care and concern, but in fact it's all about control. For whatever reason, they feel the need to control your life and destroy your self-esteem and question your own emotional health.

Many emotional abusers have suffered similar treatment at the hands of parents, friends, family or colleagues, although not all abusers were themselves victims of emotional abuse. Whatever the reason for this behavior, it is not acceptable and you do not have to tolerate it, although it can be very difficult to escape from, since the abuser may not even realize they have a problem, or if they do, they may be unwilling to change.

It is possible to recover from emotional abuse and be happy again, as long as you can let go of the past and decide on new boundaries and expectations for future relationships. You can be happy again – and indeed, you deserve to be!

Made in the USA
Columbia, SC
24 June 2022